Zen and the Art of Brazilian Sticky

ZEN AND THE ART OF BRAZILIAN STICKY
& Other Roofing Tales

by

GENNITA LOW

* * * * *

PUBLISHED BY:
GLow World

Zen and the Art of Brazilian Sticky (& Other Roofing Tales)
Copyright © 2017 by Gennita Low
Cover Photo, an exclusive by Fiona Jayde

This book is a work of fiction. The characters, incidents, and dialogue are drawn from the author's imagination and are not to be misconstrued as real. Any resemblance to actual events or persons, living or dead, is entirely coincidental.

Zen and The Art of Brazilian Sticky (& Other Roofing Tales). Copyright © 2017 by Gennita Low. All rights reserved under International and Pan-American Copyright Conventions. By payment of the required fees, you have been granted the non-exclusive, non-transferable right to access and read the text of this e-book on-screen. No part of

Gennita Low

this text may be reproduced, transmitted, downloaded, decompiled, reverse engineered, or stored in or introduced into any information storage and retrieval system, in any form or by any means, whether electronic or mechanical, now known or hereinafter invented, without the express written permission of Gennita Low or GLow World e-books.

Zen and the Art of Brazilian Sticky

LEGEND AND NOTES

People always ask me, "Why did you become a roofer?" My reply has always been the simplest explanation. "Hunger," I would say. Earlier on, my answers were paragraphs, as if I needed to justify my choices to others, mostly strangers. As if they would care the next day whether the person who did their roof was a woman or not. As if they would understand ME better if I gave them my explanation.
"Hunger."
That was a universal truth to which everyone could relate.
It explains the Self.
It explains the Id.
It explains the motivation.
But enough about Zen. Let's get to the roofing stories.

* * *

Here are the cast of characters of the anecdotes in this book:

Me: The roofer who is also an author who writes romantic suspense
RB: Ranger Buddy, rooferauthor's business partner and mentor
Crapenters: A few carpenters
BSM: Brazilian Stucco Man, a very fast talker who makes unique names for the tools of his trade, confusing others and himself in all conversations.

Gennita Low

Main BSM words
Stucco = sticky
Cement = semen
Cement mixer = semen maker
Various others that will be explained through the conversations

As a roofer, the days in the sun and rain blur into hours and hours of roof tiles and shingles. One of our favorite activities during work is singing mostly rewriting lyrics to fit our mood. I used to joke with RB, as we often do, singing "Walk a mile in my kneepads" instead of "Walk a mile in my shoes" (song by Joe South and The Believers, also covered by Elvis Presley).

The days go by. It's the people that I remember. And the stories we make of our lives.

I hope you enjoy these roofing tales as you walk a mile in my kneepads.

Zen and the Art of Brazilian Sticky

"Why is the tao so valuable? Because it is everywhere, and everyone can use it. This is why those who seek will find."

- Lao Tzu

* * *

When I first met BSM, it took me a while to decipher his funny way with words.

Brazilian Stucco Man: Oh my God, all that rot! No sticky!
Me: LMAO
BSM: What's so funny? You can't do the sticky with that rot!
Me: I know. I just know you were going to say something like that. (Still LMAO)
BSM: (frowning) You wanted me to sticky this rotten fucking thing? (waving at RFT emphatically) You're crazy! No man would sticky that.
Me: Stop! (Laughing, laughing, laughing)
BSM: I don't know why you find it funny. I tell you, rot and sticky don't go together. Sticky will fall off!
Me: (cannot speak any more because laughing too much)
BSM strode off in a huff.

Me: Come back! I'll repair the...rotten fucking thing.
BSM: I'll come to sticky when that thing looks beautiful and nice, okay? My sticky can only stay on something that's not rotten or it gets hard and fall off!
Me: o-O

* * *

The Brazilian Stucco Man Philosophy for Feeling Tired

Brazilian Stucco Man: You no happy today.
Me: I'm tired. Don't wanna roof. Tired.
BSM: Ah. I understand. I sometimes don't wanna sticky too. It's like I sticky and sticky and everyone wants a piece of me and I wish sometimes someone will sticky for me so I can smack his ass.
Me: What?
BSM: You go smack some ass. Then you are happy again. Look at my sticky today, sooo beautiful! My sticky and I are happy!
Me: o-O (This is the look I usually have at the end of a conversation with BSM)

* * *

Brazilian Stuccom Man to homeowner about his bad leaking chimney: See this sticky? It has bubbles. Water goes in, stays in, bubble-bubble. Lots of bubble.
(Homeowner looks at me. I look back)
BSM: My sticky, no bubble because water no get in. But first you need protection on top. You cover up, protect from top, no water penetration, no bubble, sticky good.

Zen and the Art of Brazilian Sticky

(Homeowner looks at me. I point to the rusty chimney cover)
Me: Umm. What he said. You need protection to umm...stop water penetration.
BSM: See? She agrees. Protection is very important for the sticky! Sometimes, it's not the sticky's fault!

* * *

Brazilian Stucco Man: I have an important announcement! When doing sticky at the beach on windy day, don't put your semen maker to face wind. I pull out my sticky and semen flies all over on a man three times my size. He kicked my poor semen maker's ass!

"When an ordinary man attains knowledge, he is a sage; when a sage attains understanding, he is an ordinary man."

- Zen Proverb

* * *

Brazilian Stucco Man: You know the big beachside job I make bid?
Me: Yeah.
BSM: It's too big.
Me: It is?
BSM: I know you're going to say it's never too big.
Me: I would never say any such thing (surreptitiously crossing my fingers). Why is it too big?
BSM: The owner he doesn't like my sticky's lie...(he looks up, thinking) ability.
Me (smile forming): Lie. Ability.
BSM: Yes. My lie-ability is no good. The job too big for my sticky.
Me: I see (trying to stop smiling).
BSM: You smile. You gonna laugh because I cannot make my sticky bizness big enough to get that rich guy (getting mad).

Zen and the Art of Brazilian Sticky

Me (really laughing now) (cannot stop): You're killing me.
BSM: You got solution or no? My brother thinks you do.
Me (wiping away tears. Really, I want to help the dude but he kills me): I cannot make your sticky business bigger but you can call your insurance to cover more liability.
BSM: Of course more! They always ask for more! My lie-ability going up to one million dollars! That is too, too much.
Me: But now you can go for the bigger jobs, see? And the rich guys won't complain any more.
BSM: It's a problem, isn't it?
Me: What?
BSM: Being a good sticky and trying not to get too big.
Me: o-O

WELL, IS THAT A PROBLEM?????!

* * *

Brazilian Stucco Man: Oh man, look at his old sticky with those things growing up and into his cracks.
Me: Hee hee. Yeah, that is a problem.
BSM: Old sticky is extra work! First you have to clean it with the pressure. I have to pressure it hard so the stuff comes off the old sticky. So many these small things, what you call them? Why you always laugh like that?
Me: It's moss. And ivy, I think. You make it sound funny, that's all.
BSM: Moss on sticky, yes. That takes hours of pressure on old sticky.
Me: You mean pressure wash.

BSM: Right. Wash and lots of pressure. Old sticky mossy is just a lot of work. Don't ever let moss grow on your sticky. Remember that.
Me: Ummm I definitely will. O-O

* * *

Ah, English. Both BSM and I speak English as a second language.

Me: Mr Billionaire Tristan, Mr Billionaire Tristan! (Okay, I don't actually call him that)
BT: Yes? More bad news, I suppose?
Me: Ummm, yes.
BT: What is it now?
Me: You need a girder.
BT: What? A girdle?
Me (not thinking): Yeah, you need reinforcement. You're missing a girder.
BT: (very slowly) I. Need. A. Girdle.
Me: It'll give more support. Right now, your wood is sagging right there (pointing). And there (pointing). A girder along the length here (making motion) is definitely needed or it'll just keep sagging.
BT: (sounding wry and weary) Ah. A girder. For support. What would I need next?
RB, my biz partner as I walk away: You've been hanging around that Brazilian too long. You sound like him talking about his sticky, except with a British accent. (I looked puzzle here). He thinks you want him to buy one of those women's girdles to support his wood.
Me (realization dawning): Ohhhh. I mean, ahem, oh dear me. Oh my. (I think I'll send Brazilian Stucco Man to explain next time).

Zen and the Art of Brazilian Sticky

* * *

True story. My biz partner, RB, likes to study at MickeyDees where many odd characters hang out. RB, an Airborne Ranger, is in his 60s now. Sometimes, his neighbor, 70 yr-old Navy Dude who also sometimes works with us, shows up for coffee. The other morning, they were buying coffee at said place and three old guys started chatting with them. The topic was inability to find good workers and how tough they were. You know...walk to school without shoes, in the snow, carrying an elephant, that sort of talk. 70 yr-old Dude: Hey, if you like, you could work with us today.

One of 3 men: Where are you working? RB: On a roof nearby. We need some laborers to help us carry shingles to the dump trailer.
One of 3 men: Well, to be honest, SON, I know I don't look it, but I'm 95, he's 93 and that young 'un there is 91. Between the 3 of us, I'm sure we could carry a shingle or two. It's the getting up on the ladder that's tricky.

I* would have love showing up to work and looking at my crew of handsome 70-90 yr olds. WHERE is my whip? Get to work, Old Man! Hey! NO BREAKS! ;P

"And when they played they really played. And when they worked they really worked."

- Dr. Seuss

* * *

"Hey, hey, you up on the roof!" the stranger yelled.

I looked down.

"Do you see a runaway boat?"

We were working by the river.

"A runaway what?" I asked.

"A boat! A runaway boat!"

...to be continued 😄

* * *

...continuing from this morning....

Me: (looking from where I was standing) I don't see anything. Hey, you see anything?
Brazilian Stucco Man, head stuck inside big, tall chimney: I see the same thing you do, leaky sticky.

Zen and the Art of Brazilian Sticky

Me: No, there's a runaway boat! (turning around and see BSM's ass in the air.) Never mind.
BSM (muffled voice): There is a what? (wiggling his ass) Run where? What?
Me: Run. Away. Boat! Never mind!
BSM: Run away? Where? Ow! Ow!
Me: What? What?
BSM: Something bit me!
Man on ground: Do you see a runaway boat?
Me (shouting): What bit you?
Man on ground (shouting): Nothing bit me! Runaway boat!
BSM (shouting): OW OW OW! Run away! Something bit me! Pull me out! Run away! OW OW!
Me (running from river side of roof to chimney): Oh geez.
Man on ground (shouting): Where are you running to? Is the boat going the other way? Do you see my runaway boat?
Me (shouting): No, I have to...
BSM (shouting): Yes! Yes! I have to run away! Help! (wiggling ass and legs trying to get out of big chimney)

To be continued....

* * *

Continuing...

Me: RB! Help BSM. I have to look for a runaway boat.
Ranger Buddy (who is hard of hearing, especially when wind is blowing like crazy): What?

Me (pointing to BSM): He needs help. I have to look for a runaway boat!
RB (walking slowly as he is getting used to BSM's craziness): Runaway goat? There's a goat on the property?
Me: No!!! (pointing to river)
RB: I didn't know goats could swim.
BSM: Run away! I need help!
RB (pointing to chimney): Is he looking for the runaway goat in the chimney?
Man on ground: Hey, you up there! You see a runaway boat?
RB: There is no goats on the roof.
BSM: Something bit me! Ow!
RB (pause): Unless it's in the chimney.
Me (giving up and walking to roofside facing the river)

to be continued....

* * *

The Runaway Boat Saga Part IV
From the roof top facing the river....

Me: What does a runaway boat look like?
Man on Ground (growing impatient): It's got green sails.
Meanwhile, Ranger Buddy and Brazilian Stucco Man have joined me, the latter slapping his chest area like a gorilla and not really paying attention as he spouted off a stream of curses.
RB: Are you still looking for the damn goat? Hey, goats can't swim.
Me: Maybe you should call the Coast Guard.

Zen and the Art of Brazilian Sticky

Man on Ground: They called me! Are you all idiots?
RB: Hey, we aren't the one looking for a runaway goat.
Me: It's a boat. BOAT.
RB: Oh. (pause) (looked at choppy water) So we don't have to save any drowning goat? I'm going back to work then (walks off).
Me (to BSM): What's the matter with you?
BSM: Giant ants. They went into my shirt and bit me. Here. Here. There....
Me: You should go down and change your shirt and wash off.
BSM: No way! There is a run away goat down there! It'll bite my ass.
Me (sighing) (turning back to Man on Ground): If I see something, I'll call the Coast Guard. Sorry, can't help you.
Man on Ground (shaking his head as he walks off) (probably muttering "idiots")
BSM: What's the matter with him?
Me (looking at him still pounding and slapping away) (I grinned): Something got his goat.
BSM: People are so funny (walking away, still slapping, pounding, looking for ants).
Me: Mmmhmm

The End

* * *

The first time I heard about ....

Brazilian Stucco Man: Can you help with Craig?
Me: Who is Craig? A customer?

BSM: No, he's not sticky customer! You know you sell with Craig. Online.
Me: Oh, Craig's List.
BSM: Yes, that Craig. I need your help. Like set account, that sort of thing. And you have to type ad in.
Me: Okay, but what are you selling?
BSM: Here, type this in for me. I don't need it for my sticky any more.
I look at piece of paper. It reads:
FOR SELL SEMEN MAKER. LOTS OF USE. MAKE YOUR OWN SEMEN!!!
Me: o-O (I suppose a sticky man needs a **semen maker/cement mixer**) Sigh.

* * *

Spring means...springy roofs. Leaping off chimneys. Climbing under small overhangs and yelling down to Brazilian Stucco Man: "It's small! About ten inches long!"

And BSM yelling back up: "I can put in ten inches of sticky, no problem! But can I get in there?"

And then realizing...I'm speaking to BSM, WHAT WAS I THINKING?

EDITED TO ADD:

Anyway, the whole day the crapenters repairing that cricket had been yelling to each other, the way they always yell numbers down to be cut:

Crapenter 1:   "Ten inches!"

Zen and the Art of Brazilian Sticky
Crapenter 2: "Oh yeah, but can you fit it in there?"

Grrr.

To accept some idea of truth without experiencing it is like a painting of a cake on paper which you cannot eat."

- Suzuki Roshi

* * *

While taking a short break during roofing, Ranger Buddy looked down from the roof and noticed a family eating dinner. We could see and hear grandma, mom, dad and another adult talking while four kids of various ages were AT THE TABLE WITH NO DEVICES nearby.

RB to me: Check that out. Isn't that a cool sight?

Me: Why?

RB: It's nice to see the kids eating with the family and there aren't any distractions. They get to have family time, enjoy each other's company, and get to hear some adult conversation instead of being self-absorbed.

Me: Yeah. That's rare these days.

Zen and the Art of Brazilian Sticky

From the ground, Brazilian Stucco Man heard yelling: Will you stop doing that to my sticky? Stop sawing! My sticky is just below your stupid saw! &^%&*!"

Crapenter: Listen, you F%^&king *&#R^&#, why did you put your shit there when you see my sawhorse?

BSM: Because my sticky is sitting nice and big here in the wheelbarrow, next to this big wall where you see this smooth sticky coat of semen. What do you think that means? Does that mean you can saw your horse here and fly your dust all over my wet sticky? No, it means you take your horse and fly your dust somewhere else, you idiot!

Crapenter and BSM: &**$G&^#**! ($*^$%%@$$!

RB to me as I gave him the eye: Well. Maybe the adult conversation was a bit of an exaggeration.

Me: Uhuh.

* * *

Ahem. I forgot to tell y'all.
//whispers....
I played with Brazilian Stucco Man's sticky yesterday. It comes with instructions.

BSM's instructions: "Here is my sticky for your personal use. Don't worry, it'll stay good until you go home. Unless you go shopping. Then the sticky won't be too good. Now, remember to pack it in the hole good and let it sit a bit before you scratch it. I can help you make it look like new. Do you

want me to come tomorrow?"
Me: //staring very hard at the laughing carpenters

* * *

(Note to new readers: BSM says sticky for stucco and for cement, he says....)

Brazilian Stucco Man: I don't know what to buy the woman for Christmas. Last year I gave her pretty necklace.
Crapenter 1: You can't go wrong with jewelry, dude.
Crapenter 2: How about some sticky (snickering)?
BSM: Don't be silly, she sees sticky every night. The other night she was complaining about it.
Crapenter 2: Oh yeah? Now why would she complain about your sticky? (laughing)
Crapenter 1: If I see sticky every night, I would complain too. Right, Jenn?
Me: I'm not saying a word.
Crapenter 2: She's a romance writer, dude. She sees sticky everywhere, then writes about it.
Me: Hey!
BSM: You are not helping! Sticky every day is not good. My woman, she hates cleaning my sticky up. I told her to leave it alone. Who cares about semen (cement) on my clothes and in bed?
Crapenters (on the floor laughing like hyenas)
Me (choking)
BSM: Jenn, do you scream if you have semen on your clothes...
Me (screaming over the crapenters' hysterical laughter): DO. NOT. SAY. ANYTHING ANYMORE!!!!!
Crapenters rolling on the floor now.
Ranger Buddy, walking into garage: What now?

Zen and the Art of Brazilian Sticky

BSM: Jenn is screaming even when there is no semen on her clothes.
RB: I'm outta here.

* * *

WHEN PEOPLE FIRST MEET THE BSM

I gave BSM's number to the Garbage Man when the latter needed to repair a hole in a wall.

Me: Morning!
Garbageman: It's a joke, right? Tell me it was all a joke.
Me (starts chuckling)
GM (big eyes): He's not real, right?
Me (chuckling harder): Oh, he's real. You talked to him, I gather. What did he tell you?
GM (bigger eyes): He told me he wanted to plug my hole!
Me: LAUGHING, LAUGHING, LAUGHING
GM: With his sticky or something! What the hell! I'm not letting him near my hole!
Me: DOUBLED OVER, LAUGHING
GM: He can't be real! I barely understood what he was saying, he was so damn fast. Plug my hole, get his sticky tonight, pack it in, make sure not too soft or he can't scratch, what the hell did he think he was coming to my house to do?
Me: DIES LAUGHING

* * *

New Crapenter helping Brazilian Stucco Man push his cement mixer: Hot day, isn't it?

Gennita Low

BSM: It's so damn hot, my semen maker broke. I'm so pissed off. Now my sticky is half done.

New Crapenter: Whhhut?

Crapenter 2: Don't ask, dude. Just get back to work.

New Crapenter: But—

BSM: Do you know anything about getting a semen maker to work? Or anyone? I only know how to beat it, nothing else.

New Crapenter: o-O

Me: HAHAHAHHAHAHA

Crapenter 2: Ask Jenn. She knows about semen makers. She's the NYT Bestseller of semen makers.

Other construction workers: HAHAHAHAHA SNICKER SNORT
BSM: Don't joke. I need my semen maker by tonight or the owner will think my sticky is not good looking. (Looking at new crapenter). Hey, maybe you know someone with a semen maker? Someone quick who can come to me. I don't want to ride downtown and pay for one.

New Crapenter: o-O

Zen and the Art of Brazilian Sticky

"When the mind is perfectly clear, what is is what we want."

- Byron Katie

***

Message left on my phone from Brazilian Stucco Man: "Hey, I can buy you cheap semen. Call and let me know how many. I see one gallon and five gallon cans. I think you will be happy with the price I get for the cheap semen. No worries, not stolen semen! Call me soon!"
Cheap semen, not stolen.
Can't wait.

***

RUMBLE! BOOM!
Crapenter: It's going to rain.
Brazilian Stucco Man: My sticky! My sticky! Cover my sticky!
Crapenter: Are you talking to me? Because I'm not paid to cover your sticky.
BSM: My semen can't get wet! I just got it smooth!
Crapenter: Neither can my wood.
Plumber: You two talking dirty again?
Me: LOL
RRRrrrrUMble! BOOoooooom!

BSM (yelling at sky): All I need is 15 minutes to get hard. You can't give me 15 minutes? It's my last batch of semen for the day! Now I'm going be late! You gonna make me call my woman I can't come home because I have to wait for my sticky to get hard!
Everyone: LOLOLOLOL.

* * *

SOME DAYS

The Crapenters' Revenge
Today an older man came over to me: Thank you! There is no water in my garage any more. You're the Queen of Leaks!
Me: ☺
Crapenter 1: Oh yeah, you should have seen how she was taking a leak the other day.
Me:
Crapenter 2: She is so not the Queen of Leaks. She's the Queen of Semen Makers.
Me: ☺
Older Man: What you say?
Brazilian Stucco Man, walking over: Hey guys! I need to borrow screws for semen. Anyone got screws for semen?
Me: o-O
Older Man: What? Screws for what?
Crapenter 1 to BSM: Sorry, man, we're all about Jenn's leaks today.
BSM: No screws?
Crapenter 2: No screws, just leaks around trees. She's the Queen of Leaks today.

Zen and the Art of Brazilian Sticky

Then they all died laughing. Except for the Older Man, who was very confused. He looked at me and I just shrugged.
Some days you win, some days you lose.

* * *

Today, A NEW WORD FROM BSM

Brazilian Stucco Man, looking at his cement mixer with a bad tire.

BSM: How heavy is my load of semen?

Me: Ahem. Is that a philosophical question?

Crapenter I: No, that's a loaded question

Crapenter II: HAHAHAHA

BSM: My semen maker is loaded. Can one of your trucks carry its heaviness?

Me: Well, it depends on how big their trucks are.

Crapenter 1: No way am I doing it. He'll go around telling everyone I'm carrying his semen maker for him.

Crapenter II: HAHAHAHA

BSM: You have a comepresser. Can I borrow for my semen maker?

Crapenters: Comepresser.

HAHAHAHAHAHAHAHAHAHA.

* * *

Brazilian Stucco Man's message on my phone:

Note: semen maker=cement mixer

"I just got a ticket for my semen maker! The police says I can't have it four feet. My semen maker isn't four feet. I don't know what he wants. Come talk to him for me. He won't come near my semen maker. Says it's too dangerous. Help, Jenn!"

Me: Sigh. (I have no idea what he's talking about this time either)

* * *

Just call me during an emergency. No, wait--don't.

To help Brazilian Stucco Man pay a fine for his ticket (extension ladder tied ON his cement mixer sticking out over four feet), I gave him a small job at my house. A very small patch job, you know. An hour's work, tops.

Note: Semen maker = cement mixer Sticky = stucco Scratch = scraping a wall before final layer of stucco (yes, it's called scratch)

Phone message.

Zen and the Art of Brazilian Sticky

BSM: Jenn! My semen maker is stuck! A big storm came by and blow up a tree from your neighbor. Big bad wood, oh, my goodness, I was standing so close to the wood but my semen maker saved me! The wind blowed and the tree blowed up and your back fence, kaboom! I'm okay, but my semen maker must stay the night. I think you better take picture of damage before I move anything. I swear I didn't cause the blow up. Hahaha. I make joke. You take care of my semen maker, okay? Don't let it blow up. And oh, I fixed your crack. Tomorrow, I'll scratch for some good sticky, okay? Bye! #StilllookingAtRottenTreeTrunk #ThankGoodnessDidnotHitBSMorSemenMaker

* * *

Today's rant, courtesy of BSM, interspersed with many stronger words in between:

"I hate cheap premade sticky! I hate cheap ready semen! Why do people not like fresh semen any more? This ready sticky uses fake semen and then they call me and ask why it doesn't look good in their cracks? Do you stick bubble gum in your crack? No! So why stick cheap fake-ass semen that don't look like my strong sticky?! I hate cheap people who know nothing! Do-it-yourself-repair-sticky-shit! Then they call me to...what...clean up their semen problem? Their cracks deserve to break bigger and bigger!"

Much throwing of objects.

I'm guessing some homeowner did a repair with the wrong kind of stucco. Not sure. I'm just glad it wasn't me ☺.

* * *

Brazilian Stucco Man: Read this! The carpenter said this says hydrogen brittle men makes my semen maker weak!
((Laughter from crapenters).
Me (looking at magazine headline and reading out loud): Hydrogen Embrittlement in Construction. Huh.
BSM: Well? Is my semen maker going bad? How long before my sticky can't come out? Read it! For me. This hydrogen brittle men sounds really bad and nasty for my semen maker! Why is there always something?!!!
(This article is three pages long. I am working. Meanwhile, the dude is telling everyone that his semen maker is going to die soon, killed by Brittle Men. Sigh. Damn teasing crapenters)

* * *

Brazilian Stucco Man and Breasts
(HAHA I knew I would get your attention. If you didn't know, it's Breast Cancer Awareness Month so this is my contribution to the cause, ahem.)

Ranger Buddy: I'm tired of all these pink breasts.
Me: Huh?
RB: Everywhere, man. I see giant pink breasts. On the plane billboards, on the cars, the other day on the news with our sheriff wearing a pink bra, and now the bank has giant pink breasts.

Zen and the Art of Brazilian Sticky

Me: Those are pink ribbons
RB: They are meant to be breasts. Why is the sheriff wearing a pink bra? Because of the pink breasts.
Me: It's breast cancer awareness month.
RB: I can't wait for scrotum cancer awareness month. Will the female cops be wearing pink balls?
Me: Heehee. Come on. You can wear a pink bra. I know a chief of police (ahem) who wore a pink kilt.
RB: A pink skirt?
Me: He called a kilt.
RB: Well, at least he wasn't wearing a pink bra like ours.
Me: HAHAHA!
Brazilian Stucco Man: I went to the bank and they were giving away those pink things.
Me: Yeah, you should get some.
BSM: I did. I asked and the woman gave me the stinky eye.
Me: Why? What did you say to her now?
BSM: Nothing! I told her I wanted to sticky the ribbon on my semen maker. Show support. I don't know why she got mad.
Me: Oh no! AHAHAHA. Oh dear. HAHAHAHA.

* * *

Inside joke gone viral: the moment when you go to the roofing supply store and inadvertently order "one can of semen" and the salesman understood and got you a can of cement. And yes, I asked, and yes, he knew the Brazilian Stucco Man.

We smiled at each other in understanding. ☺

"Learning Zen is a phenomenon of gold & dung. Before you learn it, it's like gold; after you learn it, it's like dung."

- Zen Proverb

* * *

Brazilian Stucco Man's Brilliant Christmas Idea (courtesy of me)

Brazilian Stucco Man: Why are you walking like you have wooden leg?

Me: Because I was chasing the Garbage Man.

BSM: You have to chase your men? Why? And why would he give you wooden leg? Crapenters: HAHAHAHAHA!

Crapenter 1: Because she's all about the wood.

Crapenters: HAHAHAHAHA!

BSM: Why?

Me (tongue-in-cheek): I have to give him shit.

BSM: You give Garbage Man shit?

Zen and the Art of Brazilian Sticky

Me (nodding) (I have many, many cats): 50lbs. And he takes it too.

Crapenter 2: That's a lot of shit for a wooden leg.

BSM: No, wait, you pulling the leg. But your leg is still wooden.

Ranger Buddy, walking by: I'm confused. Who's pulling a wooden leg?

BSM: I pull my semen maker and don't chase nobody.

Crapenter 1: But does that give you a wooden leg?

Crapenters: HAHAHAHAHA!

RB: (to me, accusingly) You always start this crap.

Me: (innocently) (limping off) I don't know what you mean.

BSM: You see? She walks like a wooden leg chasing Garbage Man. She shouldn't give anyone shit. Hey, how about I mix semen with gypsum and make you Plaster Semen Leg?

Me (pausing, trying to figure out what BSM meant): Umm...Plaster Semen Leg?

BSM: For broken bones. Or wooden leg. It's a joke. I never get to tell a joke.

Crapenter 1: Oh, you do just fine, buddy. HAHAHAHAHAHA.

Me: Oh! You mean plaster of paris?

BSM: (nodding) You add water, gypsum, my semen and we can make it hard or soft. Then we mold it. My brother makes lots of art things. He can mold you a soft leg or a hard leg. I can even sticky it.

RB: Yeah, Jenny, you can use it like a planter in that jungle of yours. It'll be the new thing. Everyone will want one for Christmas. Planter Semen Legs for the yard.

Me: Like a giant Santa stocking filled with goodies! I think this is going to be big.

BSM: You think so? Semen Santa stocking? Put ad to sell on Pennysaver. Buy your wife a Semen Santa Stocking. One size fits all Christmas wishes for her little garden. Also, I sticky on the side.

Crapenters, Me and RB: HAHAHAHAHHAHAHA!

BSM: What so funny? Got to advertise my sticky for Christmas too, you know!

We laughed until our sides hurt.

* * *

Brazilian Stucco Man And Porn

BSM: Hi, guys!

Zen and the Art of Brazilian Sticky

Me: Hey, what are you doing in this part of town?

BSM: I took my semen maker to the porn shop.

Me: (spitting out my coffee)

Waitress looking at us funny as she poured coffee.

Ranger Buddy: I really don't want to know this.

Me (because I* have to know): Porn shop?

BSM: That porn shop is so damn bad. They don't want my semen maker! They said no one buys semen maker at porn shops.

Me: (choking) (Waitress hanging around the area)

Ranger Buddy: So you didn't get any money for it?

BSM: (forlorn shake of head) Said my semen maker too big. It won't fit in there. They say maybe someone wants to rent it out and then they might give them my number. I was hoping for some cash for Christmas. No one wants too much sticky around now, so my big idea was the porn shop would want a semen maker, you know? Or maybe that's a bad idea, huh. Last time some asshole didn't clean it and I spent the whole day afterwards cussing and chipping semen.

RB and me: LOLOLOLOL *dying on the table

Waitress wiping table, looking confused.

RB: Damn if the porn shop won't take a semen maker, what would? (Laughing some more)

BSM: I know, right? Everyone porns their tools for Christmas. Why can't they take my semen maker? It's not like it's in bad shape. I keep my semen maker clean!

Me to RB: He means a PAWN SHOP. *dies laughing

Waitress: Ohhhhh! He had me thinking about something totally inappropriate. (She* started laughing)

BSM: (puzzled) Yes, porn is for quick cash, yes? My semen maker should make good deposit!

RB and I fell off our chairs.

* * *

Crapenter 1: Hey, haven't seen you much. How was your Thanksgiving?

BSM: Oh, eventful, my woman beat me up.

Crapenter 1 and 2: Oh-oh. Why?

BSM: Yes, in front of the pastor! The woman is mad that day!

Crapenter 1: What did you do?

BSM: The pastor and his wife invited us for Thanksgiving and we were there with their friends, you know? Then at dinner, we all prayed and we

Zen and the Art of Brazilian Sticky

have to say stuff we are thankful for. My woman did not appreciate that I thanked her second, I guess?

Crapenter 2: Second?

BSM: Yeah! I thanked her for the man-bun she gave me because when she helped clean my semen maker, it was very windy, and she didn't want my hair all stiff from my semen. I told the pastor she was cleaning up my sticky so fast because we didn't want to be late for his turkey. The pastor then went all red and...why are you all choking and laughing? It wasn't funny! Everyone was trying to stop my woman from throwing my turkey on my head! I had to protect the beautiful man-bun she made so I hid behind the pastor and the turkey flew over his head...stop laughing! Jenn, why are you rolling like that? It was not a good day. It's the man bun, isn't it? My hair is no longer in my semen maker, see? Stop. Laughing at my. Man. Bun! She called it that name!

Laughter is a great medicine. It is a tremendously powerful therapy. If you can laugh at your own unconscious, the unconscious loses its force. In your very laughter your guilt, your wounds, disappear.

- Osho

* * *

Me with BSM and the Semen Maker On The Road

This. WILL BLOW ALL BSM stories out of the water.

I was tired. BSM needed me to look at a roof, so I went with him at the end of the day. I looked at the job, talked to him about it, and got back into his truck.

Picture this. He had his huge-ass truck hauling his cement mixer. He had his BOM-BOM-BOM tuba South American music on. I was nursing a slight headache. He was chatting away while we were driving and I was looking casually at the scenery since we were on the beachside and there were Christmas decorations.

BSM: Blah-blah-blah. Then I...Blah-blah-blah.

Zen and the Art of Brazilian Sticky

Me: Yeah?

BSM: So this-and-that, and so that-and-this. Blah-blah-blah.

Me: Uh-huh.

BSM: (SCREAMING AT THE TOP OF HIS VOICE) WHAT THE FUCKING HELL!!!!

Me: (Jumping out of my skin) What? What, what? (Looking at him) What? (then seeing his side of the window) OH. MY. GOD.

His cement mixer had gotten unhooked and was alongside his truck!

BSM: That's my semen maker! THAT IS MY SEMEN MAKER! MY SEMEN MAKER IS LOOSE! MY SEMEN MAKER! THERE! RUNNING AWAY!

Me: (shouting along) OHMYGOD YOUR SEMEN MAKER! (Yes, I actually yelled out semen maker).

BSM: MY SEMEN MAKER IS RUNNING AWAY! WHAT TO DO?!

His cement mixer was traveling at the same speed as his truck, going along merrily with a fucking Christmas bow, which I'd tied, on top of it.

Me: What? Should we call the cops?

BSM's eyes were big as saucers. Mine probably were too.

BSM: AND TELL THEM MY SEMEN MAKER RAN AWAY? NO WAY! THEY ARE GOING TO ASK WHERE IS YOUR SEMEN MAKER? AND I WILL HAVE TO TELL THEM IT IS RUNNING AWAY TO THE BEACH WITH ALL MY SEMEN! AND TEN POLICE CARS WILL COME AND CHASE MY SEMEN MAKER AND ME! AND MY LADY WILL KILL ME THIS TIME.

Me: Well, we have to stop it!

BSM: You can't stop a runaway semen maker! Look at it! It's...IT'S PASSING US!!!!

Indeed it was. It went over and neatly came in front of us, merrily going away, bow waving cheekily.

Me: (laughing) Oh my God.

BSM: Stop laughing! It isn't funny! My semen maker can't run away like this! STOP LAUGHING! MY FUCKING SEMEN MAKER IS WAVING AT ME! ITS BACK IS SHAKING LIKE SOME DRUNK HAWAIIAN HULA DANCER.

(He put his head out the window and yelled) WATCH OUT FOR MY SEMEN MAKER! PULL IT! PULL IT!

Me: (dying of laughter) It can't stop just...hahaha hahhahaha...because you..hahahahahahha...tell it to!

BSM: Of course not! I'm trying to tell the cars to pull it.

Zen and the Art of Brazilian Sticky

Me: Pull over. PULL OVER. HAHAHAHAHAHA. Not pull it.

BSM: Yes, yes...(Head out of window)...PULL! PULLIT! No, no, NOOO, GoGoGOGOGOGOGOGOGO! FASTER! FASTER!

The cement mixer was slowing down now, you see, and there was a red light and a car was stopped.

Me: ArggHHHH! HAHAHAHAHA! OMG. HAHAHAHA... (I know, I was supposed to be panicking but...)

(Meanwhile, the tuba music is going BOM BOM BOM BOM BOM)

BSM: My semen is going to come out any minute now. This is not going to be pretty.

Me: HAHAHAHA. (in a horrified way) OMG. (I was choking here) It's going to crash into that car!

BSM: GO GO GO GO GO!

The light went green.

BSM: Love you! Love you, Thank you, God, Now please, God, get my semen maker to stop playing with me and let it not blow the load all over. Please, God, don't blow the load, God.

Me: (hysterical now) Please. Stop. You. Are. Killing. Me.

(BOM BOM BOM BOM BOM)

BSM: I AM KILLING YOU?! This is a disaster! My sticky--I knew I should have cleaned my semen maker tonight before I got home. THIS IS WHAT I GET FOR PUTTING MY CLEANING OFF!

Me: Arrgghh! It's changing lane!

BSM: ARRGHHHHH! My semen maker is running away again! Oh! Oh! It's going to the curb. God, please, no, don't make the semen maker crash the hotel. I promise to clean it from now on.

The damn thing came to a stop at the curb, hit the bump and splattered some cement on the sidewalk.

Me: Oh!

BSM: OH! IT STOPPED! IT STOPPED!

Me: There's no car. Quick, quick, park in front of it.

BSM: (very fast, half in Spanish, I think) This is the best thing ever happening. I love my semen maker! I love God! God made my semen maker! God is good! God is good!

(BOMBOMBOMBOMBOM)

We got the cement mixer hitched back on and had enough water to get most of the mess off the side walk. NO ONE STOPPED TO ASK QUESTIONS. NO ONE CAME OUT OF THE HOTEL. We got back into the truck and off we went.

Zen and the Art of Brazilian Sticky

BSM: You don't tell anyone my semen maker ran away! It's embarrassing.

Me: (wiping off my tears) Are you kidding me? This will make the best Christmas story ever.

BSM: I will deny! No one saw anything! My semen maker didn't run away and make me cry.

Me: God saw everything! He's so going to tell everybody you got your sticky everywhere (cackling).

BSM (looking at me): I deny! I deny! (laughing) I've never seen sticky shoot out like that.

Me (laughing again): Me neither. Can we turn down the music?

BOM BOM BOM BOM BOM!

* * *

Me: Happy New Year! Did you have nice presents?
BSM: Yes! I went out of the country. I also got presents! A calendar for my semen maker, so now I can write down sticky times and not go home late, she says, haha.
Me: (laughing) That's funny.
Crapenter: A planner for your semen maker. God, I cannot wait to read that. Better than your semen-making scenes, Jenn.
Me: (sticking out tongue) You're just jealous because you don't have semen-making times of your own.

Other Crapenters: HAHAHAHAHAHAHAHA. She got you there.
BSM: I don't know why I need to write to myself about my sticky. I know where my sticky is at all times. Here I am. Here is my sticky. I sticky the job and make sure it's good. What is so hard? I don't need no calendar for semen maker. I can work it any time I like!
Crapenters: HAHAHAHAHA.
Crapenter: Bet you didn't say that to her.
Me: I hope not! It's a present!
BSM: No, of course not. It's the thought that counts. She worries because my sticky is getting too big and too many people want me. She doesn't want my semen maker lost! It's very nice to know she appreciates my sticky business. Not many women understand how important my sticky is to me.
All of us: HAHAHAHAHAHA

* * *

Continuing today: BSM's Weekly Planner

Reminder:
BSM = Brazilian Stucco Man
Sticky = Stucco
Semen Mixer = Cement Mixer
Calendar = Daily Planner
Crapenter = Carpenter
*
Crapenter: Hey, let's see your planner for this week! It's your first week back to work!
BSM: Lots to do, lots to do! (whips out new planner) See my calendar? All filled up for week.
Crapenter: Wow. What did you write?

Zen and the Art of Brazilian Sticky

BSM: (proudly) Monday, semen all day. Tuesday, semen maker needs blow job, Wednesday, sticky hole next door, Thursday, help Jenn with big sticky, why you all on the ground? Jenn, you tell them about the big sticky you have—
Crapenters: HAHAHAHAHAHAHAHAHA...blow job, hahahahhaha, Jenn with big sticky....
Me: Leave me out of this.
Crapenter: Yeah, Jenn, you have to tell us about this big sticky you have.
Me: (rolls eyes)
BSM: It's big! It'll take two or three days of sticky. Even RB thinks he needs two semen makers.
Ranger Buddy: Leave me out of this.
BSM: It's too bad I only have one semen maker but I work it hard! One time it worked so long, I couldn't get it started again for a weekend.
Crapenters (rolling on floor even more): HAHAHAHAHAHA.
BSM: Anyway, that's why the semen maker needs the blow job first. Big sticky ahead! Got to get ready for Jenn!
Me: o-O

Life is not serious. Only graveyards are serious, death is serious. Life is love, life is laughter, life is dance, song.

- Osho

* * *

Y'all know I injured my knee last year and have been limping on and off, right? Okay...

Me: Why are you limping like me? You're walking like you have a wooden leg (he always says that about my limping).

BSM: I slipped on my semen. I made a big mess last night and forgot.

Me: o-O Ooookay.

Crapenter: HAHAHAHA. Bet you didn't expect to hear that one.

Me: I'm sorry I asked.

BSM: I'm sorry too. I cleaned my semen maker in the dark and damn, it was cold, so I went to put on more clothes and I forgot. Next thing I know,

Zen and the Art of Brazilian Sticky

whooosh, there I was with semen butt and semen face. Who knew sticky could be so cold? I hurt something and now (wagging his leg), Semen Leg! Harder than your wooden leg!

Crapenter: HAHAHAHAHA!

Me: o-O

* * *

Now you all know I limp sometimes because of my injury and if you read the last BSM post you know he slipped and is limping a bit too. This morning we were getting ready our respective stuff and we happened to be both limping together towards the garage of the house. The new homeowner and his wife came by to look at the building.

Mr Owner: good morning. You're both limping!

BSM: I slipped on my semen the other night.

Mr Owner: what!

BSM: it was dark and I was cleaning my semen maker and then I slipped.

Mr Owner: ummm (looking at me)

Me: I didn't slip on his semen.

Crapenters are snickering now.

BSM: no, I have semen leg and she has wooden leg.

Mr Owner looked at me again. I happened to be wearing my brace so I tapped on it with my hammer. It did sound like I had a wooden leg.

Mrs Owner: Oh you poor thing! I'm sorry!

They sort of turned away, embarrassed, and RB was leaning against a block. Because he has been roofing for 40 years, his knees are shot and he wraps them up every morning with tape and those gym wraps for support. Then he puts his knee pads on.

Mrs Owner: And what is wrong with you?

RB (deadpan): I have no Knees. Just at that moment the laughing crapenter tripped on an electrical cord and almost fell over the cement bucket.

BSM: hey watch it! Or you will be cleaning my semen!

Mr and Mrs Owner walked away and I heard...

Mrs Owner: are you sure These people can build our house? They can barely stand!

#sometimesYouGottaHaveFun

* * *

Man

BSM: Brazilian Stucco

Zen and the Art of Brazilian Sticky

Semen: cement

Semen maker: cement mixer

Queen of. ..: old joke

Sticky: stucco

*

BSM: Let's sponsor together!

Me: like advertising?

BSM: they do it for Super Bowl. So let's do it for NASCAR.

Me: UMMM

BSM: We put your name first because you famous. Sponsored by Gennita and the best sticky in town! How about that?

Me: ummm

Crapenters: HAHAHAHAHAHAHAHA

Crapenter 1: This car run by 100% semen.

Everyone: HAHAHAHAHAHAHAHHA

Crapenter 2: Better yet, Driven by the Queen of Semen Maker and the Best Sticky in Town!
BSM: I like it! Jenn, think of all your readers watching the race and seeing that!

Crapenter: NASCAR drivers will be lining up for that logo on their car.

Everyone: HAHAHAHAHAHAHAHAHA

Me: o-O

* * *

BSM (Brazilian Stucco Man) message on my phone.

breeze way = connecting corridor between 2 structures

"Jenn, can you come help explain to the missus homeowner that my semen maker did not bang her breeze way? Her breeze way has scars and she says my semen maker hurt it and now demands me for free sticky! The entire thing! I can't just give free sticky because her breezeway is big! She wants sticky for nothing! And now her husband wants to check my semen maker because I told him no sticky for her! Please help, Jenn."

Sigh.

* * *

I haven't seen Brazilian Stucco Man lately but a million bikers are in town so he's probably partying his pants off. Anyway, I forgot to mention, I was at a local greasy spoon and bumped into some of the crapenters and they were laughing their ass off

Zen and the Art of Brazilian Sticky

about BSM. Here is the short version, without the dirty words:

"I was at the bar last night and just as I was leaving, there was BSM's voice from the side entrance. Some big Biker Mama about three times his size was pulling him outside and he was screaming like a little girl (affecting his accent): 'I don't--no, I don't have my semen maker outside. We can't see my semen maker in the dark! I--no, really--what are you doing? I thought you want sticky job! No, sticky, sticky! Not that! Lady, lady! My semen maker isn't here!!!!'

And then he disappeared because Big Biker Mama had bear hugged him outside."

I asked: "Why didn't you save him?"

"Oh, hell no. I'm not into foursomes. Or maybe fivesomes with that woman."

The crapenters laughed and laughed and laughed again. Oh dear. Like I said, BSM was probably partying his pants off.

* * *

BSM (putting down his cement bucket): Why are you holding your hand up like deenasore?

Me: Deeno-what?

BSM: Deenasore. (puts both arms up like kangaroo)

Me: Oh. Dinosaur. (smiling because yeah, I guess I was favoring my arm) I slipped on the roof and hurt my elbow.

BSM: So now you walk like a wooden leg with a deenosore arm.

Laughter from crapenters.

Me: Umm. Okay, that's funny. You make me think of a giant wooden leg with dinosaur arms.

BSM: Haha. Yes, it is what I get when I carry too many buckets of semen. One time, I had to take it all up three floors and then throw the semen over the firewall. All day long, my poor arms, more and more semen. Do you know how hard it is to make good sticky with deenosore arms? I had to invent new sticky moves!

Me: Sticky moves?

BSM: Yes, you know, sticky moves! (He waved his trowel the way a stucco man smears a wall). Lucky for me, I'm a great dancer so, even with deenosore arms, I still can do a sticky job.

Me: I'm not sure what you mean. Like, you dance to stick--I mean stucco?

BSM: (He nodded proudly) Yes, I did the cha-cha-cha. See? One, two, cha-cha-cha, one two, cha-cha-cha. (He held his trowel against his chest like I was holding my arm and shuffled to the left at the

Zen and the Art of Brazilian Sticky

one-two beat then sort of do this steering wheel motion at the cha-cha-cha) See? It gets harder when I have to go lower because then I have to do the twist too!

Me (laughing): So what do you do when you have to stucco right by the floor?

BSM: I do the split then! Let me show you. (He tried and then there was a big RRRRrrrrrriping sound from his pants)

Me: Oh, no!

BSM: Oh, oh, oh! (Grabbing his pants and losing balance, then toppling forward and backwards, trying to catch hold of something).

Me: I can't save you! (waving my deenosaur arm)

Crapenters: Laughing like maniacs.

BSM stumbled and sat down butt-first into his bucket of cement. I mean, he sat down really, really hard.

BSM: Oh no! My butt! The semen is getting in my butt! Help me out! Help me out! Semen in my butt! Ohhhhh!

Crapenters: HAHAHAHAHAHA!

Crapenter 1 finally helped him out but it took a minute to unstuck him from the cement bucket. I laughed so hard my deenosore arm didn't even feel any pain when I accidentally hit my elbow against the door jamb.

* * *

RB (walking past me): Your turn.
Me: Huh?
BSM: Do you know anything about Cupid's feet?
Me: o-O. Cupid's feet? No.
BSM: Nobody knows anything about Cupid's feet!
Me: (trying to be helpful) Why do you want to know about Cupid's feet?
BSM: Because my woman asked me.
Me: (sighing) (Do I really want to continue?) (Of course I do) Why is she asking you about Cupid's feet?
BSM: She said my semen maker is like her washing machine and she wants to know the size of my semen maker in inches. She asked, how big? I said, it's Cupid's feet. And she asked, What's Cupid's feet. I said, that's how big my semen maker is. It measures Cupid's feet and semen makers have big Cupid's feet. She hit me on my head and called me names. Why you laughing like that?
Me: (laughing so hard I'm on the ground)
RB: What is he saying?
Me: Cubic feet. He wants the cubic feet for his semen...ahhh...cement mixer.
BSM: That's what I said! My semen maker is not in inches, it's in feet! Cupid's feet!

* * *

Message on phone:
I went to Palm Coast for a job and they told me I have to call the city for registration. So I called

Zen and the Art of Brazilian Sticky

and said I want to register my sticky. The lady asked how do I sticky and I told her with my semen maker. She hung up on me. Can you help? Maybe I need good references?

* * *

BSM made a pun today ☺. Sort of.
I showed him my two book covers, Virtually Hers and Virtually One, and he asked me why "Virtually."
BSM: What does it mean, this Virtuolly?
Me: Virtually. Well, my series have virtual reality in it and the title plays with being virtual. You know virtual reality, right? (I brought up different concepts)
BSM: Virtuolly romance? Why not try real romance? Now you write virtuo romance, all alone,
thinking inside your head? It sounds so easy. Think, boom! (He gestures like some genie) By the way, is that model's naked body in your head while you write? (laughs evilly)
Me: (laughs) Yes he is! It's all in the head, right? Even writing. It's done virtually first, see? Imagination is hard, by the way. I think I will name my next title Virtually In My Head.
BSM: Ahhh, haha, right, but virtuo is not as good as my title!
Me: What?
BSM: Virtuolly Man is okay, but I got Virtuoso Semen Maker! Which one is harder? Nothing can be harder than sticky!
RB: I think he won.
Me: Yup.

* * *

Today's roofing adventure.

Before I continue, WE ARE ALL RIGHT. We are fine.

Note: yo woman = your wife

There we were, taking shelter in the garage from a sudden storm. Sitting and standing, shooting the breeze. The house was acreage space, lots of pine trees surrounding beautiful land.

Then, suddenly...you see the bright blue light first, so sheer bright you almost need to close your eyes. After that, the arc of electricity, a streak of bright light. This thing was only 20-25 feet away. My hair literally stood up like I had my hand on a Van de Graaf generator. There was a strange WHOOOoooooosh sound too.

After that (and this happened in half a sec), the loudest CRACK! and something exploded in mid air. Every one of us jumped out of our skins.

Crapenter 1: Shit! F&^%! Did you see that?!

Crapenter 2: That was too damn close!

Me: Wow, it was blue! Did you see how blue it was?

RB: Everyone ok?

Crapenter 3: Where's BSM?

Zen and the Art of Brazilian Sticky

Crapenter 1: He was standing there rolling his hose.

Me: Where is he? BSM!

Suddenly....

BSM: ARRRggHHHH! My semen maker! My semen maker's on fire!

We all rushed out. Sure enough, the cement mixer was smoking.

BSM: ArrRRRRgHHH! It got inside my semen maker! All my semen went whoooooosh! On the lady's car!

We all rushed to other side. Sure enough, there was a hole and the owner of the house's car was...umm...covered with...

Owner of the House running out: What happened? What happened?

BSM: My semen maker! On fire!

Owner: What? Your WHAT?

BSM: My semen maker on fire! So hot it blows the whole load onto yo woman's car! Yo woman not in it so no worries my sticky didn't touch her!

Owner: WHAT? OMG! The car! That's my wife's car!

BSM: My semen maker did it! I didn't do it! My semen is on yo woman's car, but it's okay, she isn't here when my semen maker blow my load.

Owner: WHAT THE HELL ARE YOU TALKING ABOUT BLOWING YOUR LOAD?

Here is where I stepped in to get things settled down because the crapenters were laughing, RB was walking away and BSM was waving his water hose in a very suggestive manner. After the owner went to call his insurance, etc., BSM turned to me.

Me: Are you all right? Why are you grinning like that?

BSM (doing a Brazilian jig): Now I get to buy a new big semen maker with bigger Cupids feet! Bigger Cupids feet, more semen to sticky!

Me: Sigh.

And........in case you don't know, from earlier adventures with BSM, Cupids feet = cubic feet

Zen and the Art of Brazilian Sticky

A young monk brought two potted plants into the monastery's garden while the Zen master looked on. "Drop it," instructed the master. The young monk gently let down one pot. "Drop it," again ordered the master. The monk let go the second pot. "DROP IT!" roared the master. The young monk stammered, "But... I have nothing more to drop." "Then take it away," said the old master, smiling.

***

Gennita's Late Night With A Taxing Problem....

Even I couldn't decipher this BSM puzzle until just a minute ago. I've been busy doing taxes

Me: Hey, how you did you make out in the hurricane?

Brazilian Stucco Man: I make out fine! I have more men asking for my semen.

Me: (pause in the middle of doing stuff because...) What?

BSM: I have more men coming at my house for semen!

Me: (looking at Ranger Buddy)

RB: I heard more men coming, so I'm going (and off he went).

Me: Okayyyy, more men coming at your house. Did you give them any...umm...semen?

Crapenters: (snickers, stopping their sawing)

BSM: Of course. It's hurricane damage! I took out my semen maker and they took it to church.

Me: Huh. (My standard reply when I'm trying to process a BSM sentence)

BSM: It's so funny, no? More men playing with my semen maker in the wind. Do you think their wives help them do the sticky in their church?

Me: (totally lost now. Crapenters have totally lost it by now too.) I...well...maybe not.

BSM: They didn't want my help too, just my semen maker. It is good to donate my semen to church. More men love me now.

Me: Well, I'm glad. Let me get back to work. Talk to you later!

On the roof, RB: You didn't get what he said.

Me: Nope.

RB: You heard him talking about making out with more men asking for his semen.

Me: Yup. No idea what that's all about.

Zen and the Art of Brazilian Sticky

RB: Now you know how I feel.

While doing taxes, I was reading some lines about church exemptions and what not and...I GOT IT! BSM MEANT MORMON! Mormons borrowed his cement mixer. Not more men. Belatedly, AHAHAHAHAHAHAHAHAHA! Wait until RB hears this at work!

* * *

Me: Why are you all bent over?
BSM: I pulled my semen maker too hard.
Me: Sigh. (Why did I ask? Why? Why?)
BSM: I hurt myself, I pulled it so hard. It was going fine at first because I'm strong, you know, but then I move wrong way while moving around wet semen and before I know it, my back went the other way while my body moved this way. (He demonstrated)
Me: I'm sorry you hurt yourself. (changing subject) I did the same thing last week.
BSM: You pulled a semen maker too? Now why didn't you call me? You don't like my semen maker? I got a new one!
Me: No, no, I did it raking leaves and picking branches from the hurricane.
Crapenter: She probably pulled a semen maker too, BSM. She probably writes about semen makers in her books. Best-selling semen makers, I heard. (snickers from the electrician nearby).
Me: Pffft.
BSM: Oh, good! Be sure to ask me anything you want about sticky and how to make good sticky.

Me: (Obviously, no changing the subject) Why were you pulling it anyway? Why didn't you use your truck?
BSM: Remember, I told you more men love me now?
Me: (sigh) Yes. (this is from previous adventure, if you guys recall)
BSM: Well, they pulled my semen maker to their church and they then put it behind the wall to do sticky. They sticky all that and then they locked my semen maker there, with no way to get it out except to pull it all by myself! They just called me and said, (in sing-song) "herrrre, come get iiiiit" and no one was there to help me! Just me alone with my semen maker! (He gestured) Which just shows, you do a good deed and more men will take advantage of you. More men can kiss my ass next time.
Me: o-O

Notes: More men = Mormons. Apparently, BSM helped some Mormons who borrowed his cement mixer.

* * *

Brazilian Stucco Man's philosophical musing #4116:

"Always make customer happy.

When the time change, my semen maker will make noise an hour early. Must warn the homeowner's wife. She said to wake her up before my semen maker does."

Zen and the Art of Brazilian Sticky

RB: You should have just stopped at the first sentence.

* * *

Note: Love sponge = we buy cushion sponge to use on the roof to keep shingles from sliding. When they are new, they are huge and springy. We like to use our marker and write "Roofers Love Sponge" on it.

My business partner just took my napkin to wipe his face. I don't even think he noticed it's mine and was by my plate.

One of the other crapenters did, though, and said to RB, "Why don't you use her love sponge too?"

Never missing a beat, RB replied (still not knowing he used my napkin), "That requires more energy than my lunch provides."

Oh, by the way, I posted a picture of the roofers love sponge the other day. It was the talk of the job site.

* * *

Message on my phone:

BSM: My semen maker died. It is coughing and smoking too much. Why is the warranty limited for parts? Why does my semen maker need laboring? I keep telling it's not laboring I need but moving. My semen maker must move, I said. Can you explain to them to put moving parts to my semen maker?

Me: o-O

Zen and the Art of Brazilian Sticky

A hen is only an egg's way of making another egg.

-Samuel Butler

* * *

At the restaurant, with waitress standing by.

BSM: Where have you been? I was at your place.

Me: Why?

BSM: You told me you needed my semen.

RB: choking

Me: What?

BSM: To patch your crack, remember?

Waitress: coughing.

Me: When?

BSM: This morning! You told me you need sticky soon or your crack will be a hole!

Me: choking

Waitress: pretending to wipe table

RB: snorting

BSM: So where were you? I was going to give you my first semen of the year! My semen maker was ready with new moving parts!

Everyone at table: Dying.

* * *

5am
Rrrrrrrrrring

Me (checking phone to see WTF): BSM, it's 5am. WTH? Hello? Hello?
Was going to hang up, then...
BSM: Hello? What?
Me: Me, No, what? You called me.
BSM: I didn't call you. You called my name in my butt. It's fucking 5am!
Me: I did NOT call you!
BSM: Yes, you did! I heard you in my butt.
Me: What? In your what?
BSM: Butt! Arse. You were in my butt, going, hallo? Hallo? BSM? I was dreaming of the most beautiful sticky job and you disturbed me.
Me: Sigh. (Was going to hang up and then...) Wait. You keep your phone in your back pocket while you sleep? WTF?
BSM: Of course! I don't keep phone in my butt!
Me: Your pajamas has a back pocket?! (muttering) I can't believe I got butt-dialed at 5am.

Zen and the Art of Brazilian Sticky

BSM: It's shorts. I don't wear pajamas. Why are we talking about my butt? Did you call me for sticky? It's too damn early for sticky.
Me: No! Dammit, we are not going to talk about your sticky at 5am. I'm going back to bed. You go back to bed. (Muttering--probably can't sleep now)
BSM: Wait, wait!
Me: What?
BSM: I don't know why you call me.
Me: (sigh) I did not call you. Your butt called you. This is just a dream. Apparently, you have voices coming out your ass. Can we go back to sleep now?
BSM: But I can't sleep now. Maybe I can start early today. Oh, I can't. It's too dark to do anything with the semen maker. Maybe I make breakfast. Then get ready semen maker, then check sticky bags, then....
I HUNG UP.
Went back to sleep for half an hour. Gah. Who sleep with their stupid phone on them? How stupid. Coffee.

* * *

BSM: So they say my semen maker is violating City Hall.
Ranger Buddy: I'm outta here.
BSM: Also my sticky business is a violating City Hall too.
Me: Who are they?
BSM: The city. They hate my semen business and say I am violating them.
Me: Umm. Okay. Violating them? How?
BSM: I am late paying them and they say I violate them and if I don't give money my sticky will be no good for this city.

Me: Oh...Ohhhh! You didn't pay for your city license.
BSM: I am licensed to sticky! My semen maker license is good! See?
Me: That's not your city license. That's your...ah...semen maker license. Haha. (muttering to self) Semen maker license.
BSM: What's the difference? My semen maker isn't violating! How can I be violating when my semen maker isn't?
Me: Well, YOU are not your semen maker. Your semen maker is not you.
RB, walking by with tool: OMG. Now you're quoting Shakespeare or something.
BSM: Huh? ShakerSpeare? We not talking about ShakerSpeare. We talking about my semen maker not being me. So I am violating the city but not my semen maker. I understand. I'll go to the city and to make good my sticky business.
RB: God help me. (walks off)
Me: Right. You have to pay that and then you will no longer be...oh hell, why not...violating the City.
BSM: I got one more question.
Me: What?
BSM: How come, when I was arguing with that old lady in City Hall about my semen maker being good, she tells me that kind of talking is better left for someone younger than her?
Me: HAHAHAHAHAHAHA. Oh man. HAHAHAHAHA. Umm. Maybe she...hmm...maybe she was just joking.
BSM: (frowning) But I don't understand why she was joking. I kept telling her I wasn't violating the City because my semen maker is good and she just kept pushing this bill in my hand and tell me it's a $250 fine. $250 for my semen maker?! I asked. I was

Zen and the Art of Brazilian Sticky

quite upset. No, no, no, for your sticky business, she said. $250 if you don't correct the problem in 10 days. I told her my sticky business and my semen maker go hand-in-hand and she...why are you laughing like that?

Me: (on the ground, holding my tummy).

BSM: When I go next, I will tell her I have been violating the City because I am not my semen maker and my semen maker is not me and so will pay fine. Okay?

RB: (walking by again) You see what you have done now? The City will be after you for violating them with that Shakespeare shit.

BSM: I don't get this Shakerspeare joke. Shakerspeare never had a semen maker.

Me: ***dies***

People used to explore the dimensions of reality by taking LSD to make the world look weird.
Now the world is weird and they take Prozac to make it look normal.

-Bangstrom

* * *

A voice yelled out from the ground while I was hanging precariously on the roof:
"Jenn! If I tell you my sticky destroyed your love sponge, will you hate me and my semen maker? I didn't mean to be rough but your love sponge is not big enough."
Me: Sigh. (mumbling) I don't wanna know
Ground crew: #whistles #laughter #jeers
RB: That's MY love sponge. WTF did he do to my love sponge?

* * *

I'm hanging off the roof.
A voice floated up: Jenn! My semen maker tore up your love sponge. I think I need to buy you stronger love sponge.
RB: That's my fucking love sponge.
BSM: No, it's Jenn's!
RB: No, it's mine. Stop messing with my love sponge. Go get your own.
BSM: Your love sponge? Where's Jenn's?

Zen and the Art of Brazilian Sticky

Crapenter: Yeah, where IS your love sponge, Jenn?

BSM: So where do I buy love sponge for you, RB? My semen maker make hole in yours.

Crapenter: HAHAHAHAHAHAHA. How big is this hole?

Me: HAHAHAHHAHAHAHA.

RB to me: You laugh now. Wait until you have to borrow my love sponge and your foot goes through the hole his semen maker made.

* * *

Yesterdaym Brazilian Stucco Man showed up to work in his I Love New York pajamas pants.

Me: Why are you wearing your pajamas to work?

BSM: Because my work pants got semen.

RB: I'm outta here (walks off).

Me: But your pants always have cement all over. You're a stucco man.

BSM (touching his pants inappropriately): No, this is bad. My pants got semen inside it.

RB (walking by): Why do you ask? Why?

Me (laughing): INSIDE your pants? You don't mean that.

BSM: I mean that. Inside! Lots of semen. Inside my pants!

Me: How?

RB (walking the other way): I don't want to know how.

Me: Yes, you do. How?

BSM (gesturing): I was talking about my sticky and my woman got angry because she says I'm always talking about my sticky and so she put all my pants in my semen maker and yelled, How you like your sticky now? Your stupid semen maker and your sticky can sleep together! I have no idea what she's talking about. Do you?

Me: HAHAHAHAHAHA. Umm. No.

BSM: I don't understand women. So, today, pajama semen making!

* * *

BSM: Jenn, I found the solution so I don't need your love sponge.
RB: You mean MY love sponge.
Me: What?
BSM: I'm going to buy a semen maker strap to hold up my extension and another to strap down the bottom so it won't move left and right while it's shooting up.
Me: OMG.
RB: Is that how you tore my love sponge?!
BSM: (nodding) Yes, my semen maker chute--this thing--it pokes the wrong direction (demonstrating with his hands).
Me: OMG

Zen and the Art of Brazilian Sticky

RB: You abused my poor love sponge. (walks away)
BSM: What does he mean, Jenn? My semen maker didn't abuse. Just tore a hole in his love sponge. I cleaned the sticky off it really good.
Me: OMG

"You are a function of what the whole universe is doing in the same way that a wave is a function of what the whole ocean is doing."

- Alan Watts

* * *

BSM: You know what will make more money than working late with my semen maker?
Me: (sigh) No.
BSM: (showing me newspaper article on breast milk being sold, titled Liquid Gold). $1 an ounce. Breast milk makes more money than my semen. What do you think?
Crapenters: HAHAHAHA. Yeah, what do you think, Jenn?
Me: Well, first, you got to find enough women to give you breast milk, BSM.
BSM: True.
Crapenter 1: You can't just pump and sell. You have to give commission, man. You'll have all these women you have to make happy!
BSM: True. I forgot. (waving proudly) My sticky is all my own. My semen maker doesn't complain when I work it hard. Yes, you are all right. Breast pumping is not the same as sticky work. Not Liquid gold like this paper says. My* semen is liquid gold! Maybe I should use that for my ad!

Zen and the Art of Brazilian Sticky
***

Overheard by Ranger Buddy at the barber:

Barber: Gonna get you looking good for your date, young man.
Very old man: Heh heh, you make sure you do that.
Barber: So, you plannin' on making the move tonight, huh.
(All the men in the place cackled. RB said no one, except for him, was under 70)
Very old man: Planning, yes.
Another old man: He's planning, but can it still move?
Men in shop: HAHAHAHAHAHAHA
Very old man: Oh, it can still move, son. It's the rest of me that can't move.
Men in shop: HAHAHAHAHAHAHAHA

***

Brazilian Stucco Man: Oh man, look at his old sticky with those things growing up and into his cracks.
Me: Hee hee. Yeah, that is a problem.
BSM: Old sticky is extra work! First you have to clean it with the pressure. I have to pressure it hard so the stuff comes off the old sticky. So many these small things, what you call them? Why you always laugh like that?
Me: It's moss. And ivy, I think. You make it sound funny, that's all.
BSM: Moss on sticky, yes. That takes hours of pressure on old sticky.
Me: You mean pressure wash.
BSM: Right. Wash and lots of pressure. Old sticky mossy is just a lot of work. Don't ever let moss

grow on your sticky. Remember that.
Me: Ummm I definitely will. o-O

* * *

Doing a new roof on a newly-built house, first in ages.

Brazilian Stucco Man: Oh boy, a whole new house! No messing with someone else's sticky!
Me: (grinning) But you mess with someone's sticky all the time.
BSM: I know. You have to do what you have to do.
Me: (grinning wider) Yes, even if you have to mess with someone's sticky.
BSM: I just charge more, that's all. I hate it when the sticky is old and crackly, takes time to touch it and get it looking new again.
Me: (spluttering) I know, I've seen you. But now, it's a new house! No old sticky!
BSM: Yes, yes, yes, yes, YES!
Me: (laughing) Boy, you sound so...umm...excited.
BSM: You think I* am excited? Wait till you see the whole sticky crew tomorrow. They will be so excited it's new they'll be kissing the sticky. And thanking me too. Sometimes it's good not to play with old sticky, you know?
Me: HAHHAHAHAHAHHAHHAHAHA. I...can't...wait.

* * *

Lesson for the day: To avoid eye bleach, do NOT be KIND and hold the ladder for the 80 yr old man who insists on climbing up to check out the plumbing pipe in the attic. You never know if his pants has a giant hole and he isn't wearing any underwear. Oh my Lord. I need brain bleach tonight.

Zen and the Art of Brazilian Sticky

* * *

Look at him. Now look at the 80 year old man who insists on wearing pants with holes and climbing up my roof before me. Now look at him again. Now think of me holding this 25 foot ladder and trying not to look up. And hoping I don't have to. Because the wind at this beach house blows hard and the ladder sways and one tends to look up to adjust the weight of the ladder and it takes a LONG LONG TIME for an 80 year old man to get all the way up as his ripped pants flap in the wind. Not that he doesn't trust my work, mind you. He just needs the exercise. Sigh. Now look at this pic again. Now laugh, laugh away, at poor pitiful me

I was sitting on metal panels today in 100 degrees Fahr. The inspector wanted each panel screwed down every four inches even though the instructions said every 14 inches (we usually do it at every foot). By 1pm I felt like a soft boiled egg from the heat radiating back at me. By 2pm my butt was on fire. Then, lightning and thunder at 4pm. I am a charred woman.

* * *

Me to homeowner: ma'am, can you come with me to Cit Hall to sign this affidavit?
Homeowner: of course. Let me go put my earrings on.
Me: 😳 (waited for 15 minutes while she went to put earrings on. A very pretty pair of bling)

* * *

Another Hurricane Came To Visit

I had a great belly laugh chatting with RB, my biz partner, who called to see if I was still alive. He saw the aftermath of Hurricane Hugo years ago on Charleston and had always left town during any hurricane. Always.

But he always leave too late because of his tendency to work and work until the last possible second so his running off (as I jokingly called it every time) always end with the funniest stories. One year, he was stuck in traffic with a Great Dane for six hours. That story had me on the floor.

Zen and the Art of Brazilian Sticky

This time, he told me, he must have hit every county until he found a motel with an available room. I'd warned him about there being no room for a whole day, but he never listens to me so of course he ended up driving around for hours like a man who never listens to a woman (heh).

Anyway, he had finally ended up at what he called a "crack house" motel on the other side of the coast. This was the conversation-->

Indian motel owner: $40 and $5 piece of shit.
RB (who is a little hard of hearing. Okay, a lot. And accents make it harder for him) What?
Motel owner: $40 and $5 for piece of shit.
RB: (not sure what she said) $5? What?
MO: $5! Pieceofshit!
RB: (He heard "the piece of shit" but, of course, realized that couldn't be it). $5 for a piece of what?
There was another round of this and finally the MO took him to the room and pointed to the bathroom which was being drywalled or something and said, "Damage! $5 for damage piece of shit!"
RB told me the room was small, dingy, stunk of alcohol and the bathroom was worse than his car (which, if you follow my adventures, you know to be like a tool shed and closet for RB). But it was late and he needed a room.
RB to MO: Oh! Deposit, not piece of shit! (looking around). You can't possibly do $5 damage to this piece of shit, lady.
MO: Yes! $5 for this piece of shit!
So, he paid and today, after the storm, when he checked out, he said, "Thank you for the $5 piece of shit" to the MO when he got his deposit back.

I laughed and laughed until he told me he would be heading back tomorrow so we could go roofing. Blergh.

Funniest story from this storm.

* * *

Can't chat right now. No electricity and 100mph winds and wind puking branches like arrows at my house. I am fine but then who wouldn't after iced coffee and Vodka?

Best phone call this morning (had several)

Woman: I WANT YOU TO COVER MY ROOF RIGHT NOW!!!! I live at ••••••••••••
Me: It's blowing like 100mph out there. Sorry.
Woman: I NEED YOU HERE!!!!! SEND YOUR EMERGENCY CREW RIGHT NOW! I WILL SUE YOU IF I GET HURT!!!! (Cursing at me)
Me: (walking out my front door. The wind was howling like me when I sing in a wind tunnel. I yelled) OKAY I AM COMING RIGHT NO—ARGGGGGgggggHhhhhhhhhhh (and hung up the phone).
Went back inside my house to drink more coffee.
#hurricane

Zen and the Art of Brazilian Sticky

> The only thing that interferes with my learning is my education.

-Albert Einstein

* * *

Three things I learned doing metal roofs:
1. You can't sit down and write a few sentences of your story while sitting your butt on galvanized metal heated at 130 degrees Fahr.
2. You have to be willing to go up and down the ladder eight times to get one piece of metal to fit nicely in the valley.
3. Your drops of sweat evaporate fast when you hug the 130 degrees Fahr. heated panels to your chest while climbing down the roof.
3a. I hate small metal roofs with valleys and hips. Hate. HATE. Like, want to KILL crapenters kinda HATE.
3b. Wet panties dry fast on metal roof panels.
3c. Sweaty men on metal roofs are yucky.

* * *

Ranger Buddy's car was stolen at work one day. I had a book convention to attend in Las Vegas, so RB had to do a lot of paper work instead of me.

Quick Update on RB's Stolen Car →
Me: How's the car?
Him: It's very clean.

Me: Oh, I guess, they didn't leave us any tools?
Him: Nope.
Me: So we have a clean car, eh?
Him: Yup. And it's tinted. They power-washed it but couldn't get the tar off the seats.
Me: Tinted? (LOL)
Him: Yup. Like a drug dealer's car.
Me: Tinted and clean. We're gonna look cool riding.
Him: And a new boom stereo. (LOL)
Me: Hooyah! Well, no more of that crackly stereo. Hey, I'll be back Monday, do you need me to call in any (roof) inspections?
Him: Yeah.
Me: And oh, if you don't hear from me, I jumped off a building.
Him: (calmly) How so?
Me: There's a zip line connecting two buildings. Only 51 stories.
Him: So, a shortcut instead of elevators.
Me: Yeah. Only windier. So, if you don't hear back from me....
Him: I guess then I'd have to call the inspection in myself.
Me: Yup.

"The whole moon and the entire sky are reflected in one dewdrop on the grass."

- Dogen

* * *

Homeowner: I would like a new roof quote. Do you think it's time?
Me: o-O
Ranger Buddy: I think the roof still have some life.
Me: ahem.

* * *

How paperwork is effing up our world.

Today, Episode 1:

Contractor: Boy, it's harder and harder to build a house these days in this area.
Me: Why?

Zen and the Art of Brazilian Sticky

Contractor: You know how it's a law we must have a portolet at every job site?
Me: Yeah.
Contractor: Well, I got fined today because I found out now I need to get a permit to put a portolet at a job site.
!!!!!!!

Today, Episode 2:
Doctor Homeowner: Thanks for coming to check the leak this late.
Me: You're welcome. (I've been to this house before, so know the doc. She usually hands me a "natural" drink instead of soda but today...) Hey, this is Sprite. What, not giving me a medical lecture tonight?
Doc Homeowner: Ah well. I quit as a doctor.
Me: What? Why?
D/H: The paperwork was killing me.
Me: So, what do you do now?
D/H: I'm opening a cookie business. Want to try some?
Me: Where is your store?
D/H: The business isn't open yet. Apparently, I need permits.
Me: LOLOLOL
After trying cookie....
D/H: Which one do you like? One is natural and one not.
Me: This one.
D/H: Thanks for tasting! I tried to take it to the jazz festival the other week to get people to sample which one but it was a no-go.
Me: Why?

D/H: Apparently, I need a permit to let people sample.
Me: LOLOLOL !!!!!!!

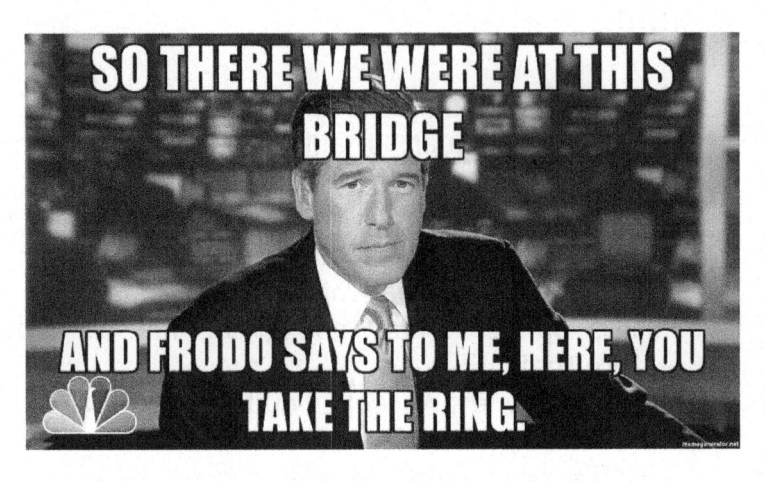

* * *

[meme image: news anchor with captions "SO THERE WE WERE AT THIS BRIDGE" and "AND FRODO SAYS TO ME, HERE, YOU TAKE THE RING."]

LOLOLOLOLOL
sips coffee
LOLOLOLOLOL some more.

This incident (referencing above meme) reminded me of a roofer worker we hired years and years ago who used to lie about not coming to work all the time. One day:

Worker: I was so ill yesterday, that's why I couldn't come.
Us: Oh, how sick were you?
Worker: It was bad. I was puking and had a temperature. I went to see the doctor. He almost sent me to the hospital!
Us: Wow, you must have been really sick!

Zen and the Art of Brazilian Sticky

Worker: Oh, yeah, I was barely able to walk in the clinic. The doctor performed all sorts of tests. He gave me a PAP smear and everything.

(Silence)
(Cackles)
RB: You had a great story going there and just had to add one more detail too many, son.

#lies #storiesgettingBigger

Still made a great story to tell after all these years. *Chuckle

"Life isn't as serious as the mind makes it out to be."

- Eckhart Tolle

* * *

I was asking everyone on the job about their smoke detectors and how to/etc. today. Here is Brazilian Stucco Man's take....
(remember, "sticky" is stucco)

BSM: It can't be hard putting it on. You put sticky on fine when you never touched it before. You'll figure this one. It's all pulling and not touching the wrong spots.
Crapenter (straight face): You hear that, Jenn? It's all pulling and not touching the wrong spots.
Me: Shut up.
Electrician: Actually, you should turn off at your breaker box first so you don't touch a hot wire.
Me: Okay.
BSM: My sticky touched a hot wire once. I passed out and then said, Wow, you know? My sticky was still in my hand but hard as a rock. Lucky for me, the hot wire just tapped my sticky. You be careful tonight when you screw stuff, Jenny!
Crapenter and Electrician now rolling on the floor, laughing.

Me: o-O

Zen and the Art of Brazilian Sticky

* * *

Yesterday, I shocked and amused a bunch of construction men. You know how I've told you, being on the roof, I see a LOT. Men tend not to think when they go back to a tree and gather around behind a bush that the girl roofing on the BACK SIDE of the house can see them doing their business.

So you know about those pee cups being on sale that has an opening at the end, so girls can pee standing up? Heh heh heh.

I filled up a makeshift one with water, and putting a finger on the hole, I sauntered over to a particular "water cooler" spot for four guys.

"Oh hey, guys," I boomed out in a manly voice.

"&%#^*!"

"Damn!"

"@!)%&*!"

And lots of zipping noises followed.

I unhurriedly pretended to unzip my pants (I don't wear pants with zips or buttons), placed the cup on where I think a penis would be hanging off and let my finger go. While I "peed," I had quite a nice conversation with men whose mouths were agaped.

"Yo, how ya doing? Hot today, ain't it? That fucking digger broke on me again and I've to use a shovel. Oh, hey, that party was great last night, man. That girl? I swear she looks like that roofer who is on the roof all the time, working, working, working. Ya think she ever notices anything? Like our dicks hanging out while we pee all over the tree trunks?"

When I was done "peeing," I took the cup and tapped it against the tree.

"It's freaking hot, man. Drink, pee, drink, pee. It's the fourth time today I'm out here. See ya next round. Have a nice one."

And I sauntered back towards the house. Climbed up the ladder that was parked against the house. Turned and waved at the last rung. Got back on the roof and turned to face the boys as I squatted down to resume my shingling.

TWENTY SEVEN YEARS, and they finally invented something to give me inspiration to join the guys for a peeing session.

#joke #slayedsomeMenAgain #pee #summer

* * *

Are you familiar with the 80s and 90s Wrestling Guys, who were on TV and always yelled like black church ministers during service? They had names like Jake The Snake, The Ultimate Warrior, and of course, y'all might have heard of Hulk Hogan. They were kind of funny to watch with all the make up

Zen and the Art of Brazilian Sticky

and superhero antics. Kids loved them. So did many bodybuilders ☺ :).

I used to get a kick out of watching Ranger Buddy, when he was a bodybuilder, imitate their stance while on the roof and scream out one of their speeches. It was all in good fun. He did it well and he was in excellent shape back then.

Anyway, recently, Dusty Rhodes "The American Dream," one of those wrestlers who had always amused RB, passed away. Dusty Rhodes was great at those speeches that rhymed and rapped. He had several phrases that I have somehow retained in my memory until today (no idea why).

Well, last night, I told Ranger Buddy I couldn't meet him for some accounting stuff because I was celebrating making the USAToday Bestselling list.

Today, when I saw him, he tried to show me off to the other workers, yelling out, "What are you today, Gennita Low?"

He expected me to yell back, "I am the New York Times and USA Today Bestselling Author, that's what I am!" like I did two weeks ago. Instead, I jumped on top of five bundles of shingles, posed like Dusty Rhodes used to do, and boomed out one of his favorite phrases, "I am The Tower of Power, The (Wo)Man of The Hour, Too Sweet To be Sour, that's what I am!"

Cracked. Ranger Buddy. Up.

So that's what he's been calling me all day. Just went to the bank.

"Hi, Ms Low, how are you today?" asked the teller guy, with whom we always joked around.

"She is more than fine," boomed RB. "She's The Tower of Power, The Woman of the Hour, and Too Sweet To Be Sour!"

"That's right!" I boomed back.

"Oooookay," said the teller.

LOL.

#aLittleFunInTheHeat

***

Zen and the Art of Brazilian Sticky

The building owner said, "My roof is leaking. Can you go take a look?"
"Sure," I said, "How long has it been leaking?"
"Not sure. A while."
Ten minutes later....I'm still laughing on the roof. You tell me what I found up there!

* * *

Homeowner: Why is my roof leaking? I just replaced it a few years ago. Can you write a report and say it doesn't look too bad up there?

* * *

My puzzle today:

You (not you, just generic) live in a wealthy neighborhood in which houses have HANGARS and there's a private air strip for your plane. You own a plane. You live in a million dollar home. You drive a Cabrera convertible. I'm assuming life is good here. YOUR ROOF IS LEAKING. Very, very badly. You have let it leak for years and years all over and your house is slowly being ruined. You contacted me and I gave you a price for an entire new roof (can't fix) and you tell me you have no money so could I go cheaper. Umm. Can I repeat the above first four sentences? Also...sell your car? Or airplane? No? Let me back out of your 100 foot brick driveway....

I'm puzzled, though. Did the owner really thought it would just cost a couple of hundred dollars to fix his problem???!

* * *

Zen and the Art of Brazilian Sticky

Owner: Why is my building leaking?
Me: because your roof is a swimming pool?

"Wherever you are, be there totally."

- Eckhart Tolle

* * *

Me: Hey, haven't seen you in a while. Where have you been?

BSM: It's been raining. You know sticky is soft when too wet.

Me (smiling): Mmmmhmmm.

BSM: Which reminds me of my current sticky problem.

Me: What.

BSM: My neighbor's sticky.

Me: Ummm.

BSM: He has a wall and his sticky is not weeping.

Me: Is not what?

Zen and the Art of Brazilian Sticky

RB (sigh): I don't want to know.

BSM: Weeping. No hole.

Me: Oh. Weep holes, RB.

RB (voice dripping with sarcasm): Of course. Sticky doesn't weep means no weep holes. How did I not know?

BSM: Yes, so the wood is now rotten from being wet all the time.

Me: Yes, I've seen this before. The stucco absorbs water from the pavement around the house.

BSM: Yes, yes, sticky sucks water all the time!

RB: Of course he would say sticky sucks water.

BSM: You are in such a bad mood. Must be all the rain everyday making you bad mood. Maybe you help me with my sticky problem? I need to repair the no weeping sticky. Do wall and bang some weeping holes. Then no more sucky sticky!

RB: I'm outta here (pays lunch).

BSM: He sure walks away fast. He's scared of weeping holes..

Me: Yup.

BSM: About helping me bang a hole....

Me: Nope.

***

Me: It's raining very hard out there. I hope you didn't try to...you did, didn't you? You try to repair your neighbor's stucco.

BSM: Oh my God, my neighbor's sticky is a disaster!

Me: Oh-oh.

BSM: His wood is so rotten. It's big! This big! (extends arms) So I got to saw his sticky higher than that. And I got the sticky off and oh, my God, termitas! Termitas eat all his wood up!

Me: Termitas...termitas...termites?

BSM (making gnawing sounds): Flying ants. (making gnawing sounds) Eat here, eat there. His old semen is holding up his wall!

Me: So what happened?

BSM: I stop part way because of the rain and the termitas. He has to call the...terminator.

Me (smiling): Exterminator.

BSM: Ex-what? Terminator! Kill the hungry ants. Then I can continue. But now it rains and rains and I told my neighbor I can't make his sticky weep hole and he said he is now weeping.

Zen and the Art of Brazilian Sticky

Me: Why?

BSM: Because I'm putting hole in his bank account instead. HAHAHA. Funny huh? I make weep hole and he weep because of hole in bank account. But his wife didn't find it so funny. She said to him to get another price. My semen not good or what? I asked her. She said, she will not argue with me about my stupid semen. I said, why you call my semen stupid? She said, I don't even know what I'm talking about. I was yelling now, I was so angry! I yell out in her yard. Not know what I talk about? Semen? I know semen! I live, eat, breathe semen! What? You tell me you live, eat and breathe semen like me? No way! You can't judge my sticky by price! You don't know sticky!

Me: o-O

Me: LOL

Me: Oh dear.

Me: What happened then?

BSM: She then got very angry with my neighbor because he was just lying on his back laughing and she threw his wood at him and say some really nasty things about his rotten wood. I have no idea she is such a bad-tempered lady. Everyone is in a bad mood these days. You should have helped me to bang the weepy hole, then maybe she won't yell like that. Maybe later?

Me: Nope.

Gennita Low

* * *

Banging the Weepy Hole Part One

(This is the first time I've ever have to use Google while banging a weepy hole.)

Me: You didn't tell me it's connected to a flat roof.

BSM: No?

Me: No.

BSM: Well, it needs big weepy hole, right? Copperhole.

Me: What?

BSM: Copperhole. You know. COP. PER. HOLE.

Me: No, I don't know. Cop a what?

BSM: To drain the weepy hole.

Me: (blink, blink) Yes...no...I don't know what you're talking about.

BSM: Drain the weepy hole!

Me: Yeah, I understand that part but what is this copperhole?

BSM: Imbornal! Imbornal! Big big weepy hole. Copperhole! Special hole! Imbornal.

Me: (Taking out iPhone) (Sighing). Im-Born-what?

BSM: Imbornal! (Spells)

Me: (Looking it up) Drainage. Scupper. SCUPPER! OH! Big weepy hole!

BSM: That's what I said! We need to bang a big one right here!

Me: (Sigh) (Mumbling: Kind deed today, remember? Kind deed).

To be continued....

* * *

To Bang A Weepy Hole Part Two

RB: That was quick. So you bang a weepy hole.

Me: Don't you start.

RB: Thought you would be longer, banging a weepy hole or two.

Me: We only did a Copperhole.

RB: A what?

Me: A Copperhole. Right, BSM?

BSM: Right, a big weepy hole.

RB: I don't want to know (walking away).

Me: Wait! It gets better. We need you for the Copperhole.

RB: No.

Me: Yup. We need you to flash the Copperhole.

RB: (sigh) It was easier when it was just about his semen maker.

BSM: There is nothing easy with my semen maker!

To Be Continued.....

* * *

Late, very late in the evening.

Part Three of To Bang A Weepy Hole: Flashing a Weepy Hole.

Reminders:
Cooper Hole—Scupper
Flashers—flashing

*

BSM: Ah! So good to see good flashers!

RB (dirty and maybe a bit more sarcastic than usual because I roped him into this freebie): It's always good to have good flashers.

BSM: And now the Cooper Holes will do their jobs! I'm glad we banged the Cooper Holes, Jenny!

Zen and the Art of Brazilian Sticky

Me: (dirty, tired, trying to stay alive) Sigh.

RB: Yup. She's weeping with joy.

BSM: And now, tomorrow, no rain! I can sticky these holes! Then I can work on the rotten wood down below before I make weepy holes.

RB: Why were you guys making these scuppers up here when the rot is down there by the pavement again?

Me: You really don't want to know.

RB: I assure you I do, since I flashed the damn hole in the dark. I want to know the whole damn story.

Me: Well, I flashed the other, so you get only half the damn story.

BSM: Now, now. We can't fight here. My neighbor's wife will be complaining about me again. He has hard time already, telling his wife my sticky is good for her holes.

RB: Do you ever stop?

BSM: Stop sticky? Never! My sticky goes on and on!

Me: *snicker. Don't take out your bad mood on him, man.

RB: Well, stop fucking around and tell me why he wanted these holes when the leak is down there.

BSM (dramatically): Leak prevention!

Me: Now he is going to go all Errol Flynn again and it's your fault!

BSM (jumping on parapet wall): This is a wall too! Para-pit also wood and same thing going to happen, so I thought AHA! What would you and Jenny do? Right! You will do the thing to prevent leak. (runs down parapet wall)
RB: He's going to fall off the wall in the dark.

Me: I told you not to ask. He's not going to stop, man. You have to watch the whole show and then praise him. He wants you to praise him.

RB: Dammit.

Me: *snicker

BSM: Low part of roof, here. (points) I said. Here one Copper hole! Then I thought, maybe then water goes there! (runs on parapet wall towards us) I said, you and Jenny will want to bang Copper Hole here too when water decides to go here!
RB (to me): I didn't know water can think like that. (mimic high tone) Oh, look, there's a hole! Let's run this way to escape it.

Me: It's logical water. Just tell him he did good.

RB: You did good. (sigh) I hate to tell you, though.

Me: Don't say it. (Because I know RB cannot stand something not done right)

RB: The membrane is shrinking all along the wall. No amount of stucco is going to cure that problem.

Zen and the Art of Brazilian Sticky

Me: *sigh

BSM: Man brain? What man brain is shrinking?

RB (pointing to all along where the edge of where wall met roof). Here! Shrinkage! It will crack sooner or later.

BSM: Man brain is shrinking!

RB: Yes! Stucco will crack later.

BSM (leaning over the wall) Richard! RICHARD! He is deaf. RICHARD!

Owner/neighbor (coming out): What, are you done? It's getting awful late, guys. My wife needs her meds.

BSM: YOUR MAN BRAIN IS SHRINKING! MY STICKY WILL CRACK YOUR MAN BRAIN.

Owner: My man brain?

BSM: YES! MAN BRAIN! YOUR BANK ACCOUNT GOING TO LEAK SOME MORE!

Owner: Let me go get the wife so you can tell her. I can't hear a thing you're saying.

RB: I'm outta here.

Me: Me too.

BSM: Look, you must let me buy you dinner.

RB and Me: NO!

* * *

And thus I'll leave you here to continue the Zen Path, listening in for yourself how this next conversation goes, when the wife hears about her husband's man-brain is shrinking and that the sticky in the weepy hole isn't the problem. Or maybe it is, maybe it is.

* * *

Sign up for newsletters: Jenn@Gennita-Low.com

Gennita Low writes sexy military and techno spy-fi romance. She also co-owns a roof construction business and knows 600 ways to kill with roofing tools as well as yell at her workers in five languages. A three-time Golden Heart finalist, her first book, Into Danger, about a SEAL out-of-water, won the Romantic Times Reviewers Choice Award for Best Romantic Intrigue. Besides her love for SEALs, she works with an Airborne Ranger who taught her all about mental toughness and physical endurance. Gennita lives in Florida with her mutant poms and one chubby squirrel.

To learn more about Gennita, visit www.Gennita-Low.com, www.rooferauthor.blogspot.com and www.facebook.com/gennita

Zen and the Art of Brazilian Sticky

Other Books by Gennita Low

BIG BAD WOLF

~ ~ Crossfire Series ~ ~
PROTECTOR
HUNTER
SLEEPER
HER SECRET PIRATE (short story)
WARRIOR

~ ~ Hot Spies Series ~ ~
DANGEROUSLY HOT
SIZZLE

~ ~ Secret Assassins (S.A.S.S.) ~ ~
INTO DANGER
FACING FEAR
TEMPTING TROUBLE

~.~.Super Soldier Spy ~ ~
VIRTUALLY HIS
VIRTUALLY HERS

~ ~Sex Lies & Spies~ ~
DANGEROUSLY HOT
SIZZLE

~ ~Susan Stoker's Special Forces (Kindle World)~ ~
NO PROTECTION

~ ~Cristin Harber's TITAN World~ ~
EDGE OF TEMPTATION

Gennita Low

~ ~Liliana Hart's MacKenzie Series~ ~
WICKED HOT

* * *

~ ~Non-Romance~ ~
A SQUIRREL CAME TO STAY

Made in the USA
Coppell, TX
11 December 2021